RAIL 3 PORTFOLIOS

The Deltics

Compiled by
Murray Brown

Copyright © Jane's Publishing Company Limited 1985

First published in the United Kingdom in 1985 by
Jane's Publishing Company Limited
238 City Road, London EC1V 2PU

ISBN 0 7106 0339 8

Typeset by Netherwood Dalton & Co Ltd, Huddersfield

Printed by Netherwood Dalton & Co Ltd,
Huddersfield

JANE'S

Cover illustrations

Front: Line-up at York depot on 5 November 1981 of the four Deltics
nominated to work the farewell specials marking the end of the class.
To many they need no introduction, but from left to right are: 55015
Tulyar, 55022 *Royal Scots Grey*, 55009 *Alycidon* and 55002 *King's Own
Yorkshire Light Infantry*. (*Murray Brown*)
Yashica 124G Ektachrome 64 1/125, f8

Rear: Deltic D9018 *Ballymoss* one mile south of Thirsk on 1A35, the
southbound 'Flying Scotsman' in the summer of 1962. This
comparatively rare view shows the dark background-style headboard
used on this service before the 'winged thistle' version was introduced.
(*Ernest Sanderson*)
Agfa Karat Perutz C18 1/500, f4

This page: Memories of Finsbury Park during the last months of the
class, with (right) the first built, No 55022 *Royal Scots Grey*, and
former Gateshead veteran No 55017 *The Durham Light Infantry*. 22
October 1981. (*Geoff Cann*)

Introduction

There has been no other British diesel class which had such an impact on the services it operated than did the English Electric-built Type 5 production Deltics. The fleet of 22 were, for most of their existence, shared amongst the depots at Haymarket, Gateshead and Finsbury Park, although administratively throughout their careers they were controlled from the Eastern CM&EE HQ at Doncaster and later from the 'new' Eastern Region at York from 1967.

Each locomotive cost £156 000 and the Deltics shared a strange distinction with the Metrovick Co-Bo locomotives in that they were the only two-stroke engined main line diesel classes to work on BR.

Throughout their lives, extraordinary arrangements were for their 'shopping' to Works where, until the mid 1970s, they were given priority. For the first eight years of the Deltics' 21-year reign, the phenomenal and complex Napier 18-25B power units were overhauled by their makers and an elaborate contract was operated whereby a joint panel comprising BR and EE staff assessed failures, attributing responsibility and incurring penalties. From 1970 BREL Doncaster took on the overhaul of all Deltic components. Initially, Deltics were overhauled at six-month periodicity (with careful provision made not to shop any during the summer timetable duration) but this timescale was gradually extended as the years passed to 18 months, with one locomotive, No 55015, as a trial extended to two years.

Ironically, for many years this legendary class could not be exploited to its full potential and it was only in the 1970s, with the abolition of speed restrictions and the introduction of multiple aspect signalling that the Deltics began to be used to their ability. Even so, timings were well within their stride and it was not until the days of 'The Hull Executive' (at the time Britain's fastest train) and the Kings Cross-York semi-fast services (totally inappropriately named) that the Deltics found schedules which were in keeping with their performance.

On 20 March 1978 the first Deltic diagram was handed over to a HST and the Deltics' days were numbered. The fleet was progressively withdrawn from January 1980, culminating in the final Deltic-hauled special on 2 January 1981, an event accompanied by unparalleled scenes of adulation and sadness.

Six Deltics have been spared the torch for future generations to savour in awe. This book remembers these six and their sixteen shedmates, from green to blue, from the ages of one to twenty-one.

We gratefully acknowledge the photographers who have made this portfolio a just appreciation of an astonishing locomotive class which, surely, will never be emulated.

MURRAY BROWN
Werrington, Peterborough
November 1984

Opposite: Deltic double-headers were a very rare occurrence and were usually only arranged to test a locomotive after attention. Such a situation is presumed to have arisen on 8 June 1972, when the 1629 Doncaster-Kings Cross was placed in the care of Nos 9019 *Royal Highland Fusilier* and 9002 *King's Own Yorkshire Light Infantry*. The pair are leaving Peterborough. *(Colin Ding)*
Microcord Ektachrome 200 1/300, f8

Below: In the last few years of the Class 55s' reign, one of the diagrams incorporated the 0940 Edinburgh-Plymouth as far as York, from where the Deltic returned to Edinburgh on the 0725 from Plymouth (1435 ex-York). Here No 55004 approaches York in the twilight of its life with the southbound Plymouth working near Overton on 21 December 1980. No 4 was condemned on 28 October 1981 after having failed at Liverpool with the 1550 from York. *(David Stacey)*
Pentax MX Kodachrome 25

2

This is Marholm crossing, just north of Werrington Junction, Peterborough on Wednesday 9 May 1962. On the left, D9020 heads south with the 'Queen of Scots' Pullman which it took over at Leeds Central at 1638. Approaching is the 1725 Kings Cross to Leeds and Harrogate 'Yorkshire Pullman' with D9000 in charge. The two Pullmans are on the site of Werrington water troughs. All the Deltics were fitted with water scoops to replenish their steam heating boilers but the equipment gave much trouble and the scoops were eventually removed. However, one Deltic still retains its scoop equipment – the prototype Deltic now housed in the Science Museum, South Kensington.

Just over one month after this photograph was taken, both these Deltics were in the limelight on 18 June hauling the north- and southbound centenary 'Flying Scotsman' trains – see pages 8 and 9. *(Colin Ding)*
Microcord Ektachrome 200 1/300, f8

Opposite
Memories are made of this. D9007 *Pinza* forges past Holloway with the 'Harrogate Sunday Pullman' on 9 June 1963. ECML Pullman services were still utilising the straight-sided Pullman brake vehicles at this time, but these would soon be replaced by Mk 1 BG vehicles which spoilt the look of the train. *(Rodney Lissenden)*
Rolleiflex 4×4 Agfa CT18 1/500, f3.5

1961 was the year of Deltics on test and both Nos D9003 *Meld* and D9001 *St Paddy* were used on various trials for timing and braking purposes. This picture shows No D9003 at Leeds Central on 18 July 1961 on a timing trial prior to the introduction of 'The West Riding'. Leeds Central closed on Saturday 29 April 1967 when the remodelled and resignalled former Leeds City station took over all Central's services. *Meld* had just received its nameplates at the time of this picture and many years later, on 27 November 1978, one of *Meld*'s plates was removed and sent to BR's Plastic Department Unit at Derby to assess if plastic replicas were a proposition as it was felt that the Deltics' nameplates were highly likely to be stolen in view of their value. However, the idea was not carried out and *Meld* had its plate refitted. (*Gavin Morrison*)

Zeiss Contaflex Agfa CT18 1/250, f3.5

1A35 and 1S17 rank as the best remembered headcodes on the East Coast Main Line – the south- and northbound 'Flying Scotsman' services. A sight probably more rare than the famous winged thistle emblem carried by this legendary train, the white nameboard was carried, it is believed, only during the first year of the Deltics' takeover of the ECML. This is Haymarket's D9006 at full stretch on that superb and beautifully aligned racing track, the 44.1 miles from Darlington to York. The location is one mile south of Thirsk. D9006 was the only Deltic to be renumbered at other than its home depot (apart from those renumbered in Doncaster Works), Gateshead obliging with No 55006 on 6 March 1974. (*Ernest Sanderson*) *Agfa Karat Perutz C21 1/500, f5.6*

18 June 1962 was a special day in the annals of ECML history for apart from the introduction of the full Deltic timetable, with vast improvements in schedules, it was also the centenary of the famed 'Flying Scotsman'. To mark these occasions, Finsbury Park 'bulled up' their favourite machine, No D9020 *Nimbus*, to a condition many people say was never bettered in the twenty years of Deltic running. Meanwhile, Haymarket had spruced up D9000 for the southbound run and it was given a ceremonial send-off by being named *Royal Scots Grey* at Waverley. The two 'ten o'clocks' are seen passing Barlby, Selby on their memorable runs. (Both: *Ernest Sanderson*) *Agfa Isilette Ektachrome 1/500, f4.5*

The first Deltic was already blue at the time of this picture, 28 April 1967, as D9021 accelerates away from Leeds at Wortley South Junction with an up express. This machine managed to survive to the last day, albeit on one power unit. (*Gavin Morrison*)
Zeiss Contaflex
Agfa CT18 1/500, f3.5

D9000 climbs past Beeston on the outskirts of Leeds on 29 June 1965 with an up afternoon express for Kings Cross. This was the only Deltic to be fitted with a xenon tube flashing headlight centrally sited immediately above the bufferbeam. Trials were conducted in March 1961 on the main line in the Kings Cross Division but it was not considered successful and the lamp was removed and the gap plated over. All 22 Deltics were wired for this lamp but it was not until nearly two decades later that BR finally opted for a quartz warning lamp and by this time the Deltics' days were numbered. (*Gavin Morrison*)
Zeiss Contaflex
Agfa CT18 1/500, f3.5

Transition time for the Deltics as green gave way to blue. Posing on York shed yard in September 1968 is No D9014 *The Duke of Wellington's Regiment*. On the left is No D8309, one of the last batch of Class 20s to be built, of which York received Nos D8300-09. D9014 was the final Deltic to be repainted blue, making its way to Doncaster Works from Gateshead for overhaul and that purpose on 27 October 1969. (*Ernest Sanderson*)
Agfa Karat Kodachrome II 1/100, f8

Berwick upon Tweed on 27 March 1977. Entering with the 1000 (Sun) Edinburgh-Kings Cross is No 55010 *Kings Own Scottish Borderer*. This was the final year of complete Deltic domination on the ECML, although by this time the power unit repair position at Doncaster Works was beginning to cause poor availability problems, with Deltic-rostered trains having to be Class 47-hauled.

Berwick was the home of the regiment after which No 55010 was named and one of the Deltic's nameplates was presented to the regiment in 1984. No 55010 survived nearly to the conclusion of the Deltics' reign but failed on Stoke Bank when working the 2300 Kings Cross-Leeds on 23 December 1981. It was assisted to Doncaster by No 47458 and ironically but ignominiously pushed by No 55019 into Doncaster Works, where it was cut up in May 1982. *(Peter J Robinson)*
Pentax 6×7
Ektachrome 200
1/500, f6.3

This 1978 view of Doncaster has changed considerably in recent years. Bridge Junction signal box has been swept away under the Doncaster power box resignalling scheme and the track layout simplified. On 23 May 1978 No 55018 *Ballymoss* was heading the 1540 Leeds-Kings Cross. *Ballymoss* entered service on 24 November 1961 and lasted until 12 October 1981. It was broken up in Doncaster Works in January 1982. (*John S Whiteley*)
Pentax SP Kodachrome 25 1/250, f4

Powering south of Retford on the 1 in 200 past Gamston is No 55019 *Royal Highland Fusilier*, in charge of an up express on 9 July 1974. This Deltic spent its life at Haymarket until transferred to York in 1979. It was the last Deltic to be named and this took place at Glasgow Central on 11 September 1965. No 19 was the second Deltic to undergo a general overhaul, only one of five to do so. Its claim to fame is that it had the distinction of powering the final ordinary service train on 31 December 1981, the 1630 Aberdeen-York, which it worked from Edinburgh. On 4 January 1982 No 19 was towed to Doncaster with sisters 55021 and 55007 by No 46009, the Class 46 that was deliberately wrecked in July 1984 in the futile smash with an empty nuclear flask. 55019 is now lovingly cared for by the Deltic Preservation Society on the Moors Railway and worked the inaugural Deltic preservation train, the 1055 from Grosmont to Pickering on 21 August 1982. *(Hugh Ballantyne)*
Leica M3 50 mm Summicron
Kodachrome 25 1/500, f2.8
Right: No 55005 was delivered new as No D9005 on 29 June 1961. It was named *The Prince of Wales's Own Regiment of Yorkshire* at York on 8 October 1963 and remained a Gateshead-based machine until May 1979, when it moved to York. On 28 January 1981 No 55005 worked its last duty, a Kings Cross-Aberdeen train, condemnation following shortly after on 8 February. A trip to Stratford ensued to allow 55005 to yield its bogies to 55021, but nearly two years elapsed before the locomotive's appointment with the torch at Doncaster in January 1983. Corby Glen is the setting for this view of 55005 on 4 June 1980. *(Hugh Ballantyne)*
Hasselblad 2000FC f2.8 Zeiss
Agfa CT18

No 55008 *The Green Howards* leaves Stoke Tunnel on 25 July 1981 with the 1403 Kings Cross-York. This was the train which should have been No 55008's last duty on the final service day. The 'York stoppers', as they were known, were tightly timed and the Deltics had little scope for delay as the following HST which left Kings Cross 57 minutes later was just behind the stopper at York. *(Rodney Lissenden)*
Pentax 6×7 200 mm Takumar
Ektachrome 200 1/500, f5.6

Pictured at Dudley, Northumberland on 22 March 1978 is No 55015 *Tulyar* powering the 1600 Edinburgh to Kings Cross, 'The Talisman'. Despite this locomotive being one of the most popular Class 55s, when it was put out to tender after withdrawal, there were no takers. A second attempt again brought no response and then No 15 had to suffer the bizarre spectacle of being auctioned at Christies on 16 December 1982. Bidding reached £5500, short of the reserve price placed on the locomotive by BR. One of *Tulyar's* nameplates was sold for £900 and the other was officially presented to the Works Manager, Doncaster where it is now mounted on the conference room wall. *Tulyar* was eventually saved by Peter Sansom, a Leicestershire haulage contractor. It was the sixth and final Deltic to be spared the torch. (*Mrs D A Robinson*)

Pentax 6×7 Ektachrome 200 1/500, f4

Opposite. Enjoying its last few days in BR revenue-earning service is No 55022 *Royal Scots Grey*, pictured at Ordsall Lane, Salford on 17 December 1981. With a mixture of Mk 1 and 2 rolling stock, the Deltic is heading the 1305 Liverpool-York service. Following its memorable last journey on 2 January 1982, No 55022 had to wait another one and a half years before it arrived on the Nene Valley Railway on 8 September 1983 to begin its second career, in preservation and bearing its former number 9000. It is now owned by the 9000 Locomotive Limited. (*Gavin Morrison*)
Pentax SP1000
Kodachrome 25
1/500, f3.5

Left. Many photographers regard the ECML north of Darlington as the most photogenic part of the route. This is Plawsworth viaduct near Durham being crossed by No 55014 *The Duke of Wellington's Regiment.* This was a Gateshead-based machine for most of its existence, finally being allocated to York with its surviving sisters in May 1979. Its withdrawal from service on 16 November 1981 with a defective traction motor brought about its condemnation on the following Sunday, November 22, and it angered many Deltic fans that such a trivial fault was used to condemn a member of this class. No 14 was towed to Stratford by 55002 on 24 November and was towed to Doncaster on 6 December. It finally met its end in February of the following year. (*John Hunt*)
Pentax SP Kodachrome 25

Exit from Edinburgh: a smoky departure from the Scottish capital is the prelude to 5½ hours of audio and atmospheric entertainment! Fittingly this locomotive will always be remembered as a Haymarket machine, although it was transferred to York with the rest of Haymarket's Deltics in May 1979. No 55006 is pictured leaving Waverley on 27 September 1980 with the 0912 Dundee-Kings Cross. It was the fourth Deltic to be condemned together with No 55005 on Sunday 8 February 1981. It had been stopped a week earlier but reinstated for one week. Its final revenue-earning train was the 1S77 overnight from Kings Cross on 4 February after which it ran light to Gateshead. After spending a day here on static crew training, it ran to York where its one operational power unit, No 415 (now in preservation), was turned off for the last time at 2030. By November 1981 the *Fife and Forfar Yeomanry* was but a memory. (*J S Mattison*) *Canon AE1 Kodachrome 64 1/250, f4*

Beside the Northumberland coast, an obligatory view, but a delightful one for a Deltic study is the Royal Border Bridge at Berwick upon Tweed. Heading the 0705 Edinburgh-Kings Cross on 29 July 1978 is No 55019 *Royal Highland Fusilier*. On this date there were no fewer than ten Deltics receiving attention in Doncaster Works. Also by this time, the Deltic Preservation Society was rapidly gaining members and funds, but they did not know that No 55019 one day would be theirs. (*Hugh Ballantyne*)
Hasselblad 2000FC f2.8 Zeiss
Agfa CT18 1/250, f4.5

Right. The power behind the button! This is power unit No 435 complete with main and auxiliary generators lying on 'The Plant' floor on 21 May 1978. The total assembly weighs 11 tons and this unit has just been removed from No 55015 *Tulyar* after four days previously putting a piston through the side of the crankcase – known in the trade as 'putting a leg out of bed'. There were 57 Napier-built power units in total which, of course, included 14 spares for the 22 Deltics. Doncaster Works began maintaining them in 1970 when the contract with Napier expired. This particular unit ended its days in No 55017 from which it was removed on 16 February 1981 after accumulating 5000 engine hours life. *(Hugh Ballantyne)*
Leica M3 50 mm Summicron Kodachrome 25 1/30, f2.8

Left. No 4 Bay in the Crimpsall shops was where the Deltics were placed for unclassified (unforeseen), classified (planned overhaul) repairs or rectification (remedial attention to incomplete or unsatisfactory work). When the Deltics bowed out of service, overhaul periodicity had been extended to 18 months, although No 55015 had been allowed to run for two years with an intermediate bogie swap to assess if the locomotive could run for this length of time. It could, but the price was high with extra work required to cater for this increased service time. This picture shows No 55002 undergoing a Light overhaul on 2 February 1980 with Nos 37089 and 50019 for company. *(David Stacey)*
Pentax KX Kodachrome 64 1/60, f4

Right. A remarkable view of a Deltic cab, achieved by means of a 15mm lens. The Deltics had very small cab areas which often gave the casual visitor the impression of danger. Curiously, spacious cabs convey the opposite impression. Considerable efforts were made in the formative years to deaden the noise levels experienced in the cabs of these locomotives, including the use of thick insulation material and the provision of a heavy duty plastic door covering which was hooked over the gangway entrance to the cab. This cab belongs to a Deltic which survived the cutter's torch, No 55015 *Tulyar*, and was taken inside York depot in the last week of No 15's BR service life. *(Brian Cooke)*
Nikon EF Kodachrome EPR 135 1 sec, f8

Above. To celebrate HM The Queen's Silver Jubilee in 1977, BR bestowed the name 'The Silver Jubilee' on the 0800 Kings Cross-Edinburgh and the 1500 return working. For the inaugural northbound train, it was the turn of Finsbury Park's No 55012 *Crepello* to bask in the limelight and in the sun as it approaches Doncaster near Bridge Junction on 8 June 1977. Twelve of these headboards were made and are now valuable collectors' items. No 55022 worked the first southbound service. (*Gavin Morrison*)
Pentax SP1000 Kodachrome II 1/250, f3.5

Right. The southbound working of 'The Silver Jubilee' was the 1500 off Edinburgh and this view depicts No 55013 *The Black Watch* passing Benton Quarry on the approaches to Newcastle on 3 August 1977. Few of these headboards survive but one is displayed on the wall in the Regional Mechanical & Electrical Engineer's office in Hudson House, York whilst one more was repainted and made into 'West Highland Tours' and carried by the locomotive, usually No 37081, on the popular Sunday Edinburgh to Oban excursions in 1983/84. (*Peter J Robinson*)
Pentax 6×7 Ektachrome 200 1/1000, f3.5

24

A study of travel-worn Nos 55010 and 55017 in the last few weeks of their BR service at Finsbury Park on 23 October 1981. No 55010 was the first Deltic to reach two million miles in December 1972, when it was still numbered 9010. Each Deltic took approximately seven years to run one million miles – a remarkable achievement and one previously unknown, but even this has been eclipsed by the HSTs which are taking four to five years to reach the same figure. Mileage records were religiously maintained until 27 March 1976, when the BR Accountant decreed that there was no longer a requirement for such figures. However, unofficial figures were certainly kept to enable a total mileage for the class to be tabulated and the staggering total of 63 million for the 22 locomotives is a fitting epitaph for the legendary Deltics. The locomotives which made it to the end of 1981 had each run 3¼ million miles. (*Geoff Cann*)

Pentax MX Kodachrome 64 1/125, f8

No 55015 *Tulyar* received its white window surrounds during a repaint at Finsbury Park on Thursday 12 July 1979. Here the sparkling *Tulyar* carries the final symbol of Finsbury Park's involvement with prestige train running – 'The Hull Executive'. This view was taken on 14 July 1979 at Stratford. *(Geoff Cann)*
Praktica TL2 Kodachrome 64 1/125, f8

Above. The scene is Retford on 20 March 1981. The train is the 1205 Kings Cross-Hull and the locomotive is No 55012 *Crepello*. Two months later it was condemned, having been withdrawn at Finsbury Park whilst undergoing repairs. It was towed to York to yield spares and then to Doncaster on 15 June 1981, hauled by No 55014. Whilst the other Finsbury Park Deltics had their white window surrounds painted out when transferred to York depot, No 12 carried them all the way to Doncaster Works scrapyard, where it was broken up in September 1981. *(Geoff Cann)*
Pentax MX Kodachrome 64 1/250, f5.6

Right. This is No 55003 *Meld* erupting into life at Kings Cross station on 16 June 1979 after arrival with the 1245 from Hull. *Meld* was the first of the Finsbury Park fleet to have its window surrounds painted white, a modification which later became the trademark of the depot's Deltics. The painting took place on 6 April 1979. Shortly after No 55015 had been similarly painted, the then BRB Chairman Sir Peter Parker visited the depot and was shown the revised style. If the Chairman approves, who can say 'no'? Finsbury Park Depot Manager Allan Baker undertook the painting in order to boost staff morale and pride during a difficult time as the depot was wound down in favour of HSTs. *(Hugh Dady)*
Praktica IV Kodachrome 25 1/5, f5.6

The National Railway Museum provided many of its varied collection of coaching stock vehicles to take part in the Rainhill celebrations, staged in May 1980 to commemorate the 150th anniversary of the Liverpool and Manchester Railway's famous locomotive trials. No 55015 had the job of hauling the stock which made for a rare and colourful picture. The special left York on 21 May 1980 and the train is seen waiting to depart from York Yard North at 1015 with the British Sugar Corporation factory in the background.
(*David Stacey*)
Pentax MX Kodachrome 25 1/250, f4

Above. It is not widely known that No 55015 was the *fourth* choice of locomotive to participate in the Rainhill celebrations which took place on 24-26 May 1980. Initially No 55013 was chosen as it was the latest to be repainted. However, No 55019 was expected to be released from Works one week before the event and even had its power units cleaned in case it was on exhibition. No 55005 was then suggested as it was thought that the HRH Prince of Wales might be in attendance but *Tulyar* won the day, although only just. York depot staff had been cleaning No 55013 until it presented an astonishing sight which made *Tulyar* look dull in comparison and it is true to say that York depot staff were bitterly disappointed that their No 13 was overlooked. Here is *Tulyar* parading in front of millions – the television cameraman can be seen to the right – on 24 May. (*Peter J Skelton*)
Contax RTS Kodachrome 25 1/250, f2

Right. Locomotives which participated in the Rainhill junketings on 24-26 May 1980 were duly fitted with commemorative plaques. The Deltic Preservation Society approached BR with the suggestion that No 55015 should also be decorated and at a small ceremony inside Finsbury Park on 17 March 1981, *Tulyar's* plaque, provided at the DPS's expense, was unveiled by Divisional Maintenance Engineer Neville Davies. When No 55015 was withdrawn, the indicator panel with plaque was presented to the DPS but with the eventual purchase of the locomotive for preservation, the DPS committee decided in November 1984 that the plaque could be reinstated on *Tulyar's* nose end. (*Gavin Morrison*)
Pentax SP1000 Kodachrome 25 1/250, f2.8

Left. Such was the enthusiasm of Deltic fans in the final weeks that every opportunity was taken to photograph every movement, even during the night. In arctic conditions, No 55009 *Alycidon* sits in No 3 bay platform at York on 16 December 1981 with the 2019 stopper to Kings Cross. This working was the last of the day-time all stations 'semi-fast' services. (*Barry Plues*)
Pentax SP1000 Ektachrome 200
10 secs, f5.6

Above. No 55009 *Alycidon* pauses at York on the 1A40 Newcastle-Kings Cross mails on the night of 30 December 1981, its last revenue earning run before the final Deltic special on 2 January 1982, when this locomotive was the standby machine and ran from Peterborough to Newcastle and back in front of the 'Deltic Scotsman Farewell'. (*Barry Plues*)
Pentax SP1000 Ektachrome 200 18 secs, f5.6

Above. On one of the first occasions a Deltic was rostered to work a special, No D9007 *Pinza* pulls out of the remote Riccarton Junction for Edinburgh on 4 January 1969 with an RCTS excursion marking the end of the Waverley route, which closed with effect from 6 January. The train had travelled from Leeds via the Settle and Carlisle line. *Pinza* faced difficulties leaving Riccarton Junction after malevolent parties placed grease on the line for several hundred

yards, no doubt in protest against the impending controversial closure. *(H C Robinson) Retina IIc Kodachrome II*

Right. It was perhaps inevitable that No 55002 *King's Own Yorkshire Light Infantry*, having been painted in two-tone green for the National Railway Museum, would be one of the four nominated Deltics to work railtour specials. Undoubtedly its most interesting outing took

place on 2 August 1981, just before its nomination, when it worked a BR-organised special from Newcastle to Whitby, the first occasion that a Class 55 had ventured down the Esk Valley line. Such was the success of this train that a duplicate was run three weeks later. Here No 2 approaches Middlesbrough with the lifting bridge in the background on the first occasion that No 2 visited Whitby. *(Gavin Morrison) Pentax SP1000 Kodachrome 25 1/250, f3.5*

Left. A real memory now as the route has passed into history for this location is just south of Chaloners Whin Junction, York, on the section to Barlby Junction, Selby which was closed on 23 September 1983 with the opening of the Selby Diversion. The locomotive is No 55002, one of the five Deltics to be given a general overhaul in the late 1970s. Its last run in blue livery was on 27 October 1969, when it was trialled on the Doncaster Works test train before being painted green at the expense of the Friends of the National Railway Museum. No 55002 is working the Sunday 1550 York-Kings Cross on 12 October 1980. *(John S Whiteley)*
Pentax SP2 Kodachrome 25 1/250, f4

Above. No 55002 *King's Own Yorkshire Light Infantry* departs from York's platform 3 bay with the 1A35 1215 York-Kings Cross semi-fast on 6 November 1979. *KOYLI* received its name at a ceremony on platform 14 at York on 4 April 1963. It was the first Class 55 to be outshopped in blue livery, so heralding an end to what many regard as the finest livery ever to be carried on a British locomotive class. *(Dave Stacey)*
Pentax MX Kodachrome 25 1/250, f4

Left. The Deltics' use on the Hull line delighted photographers, for the chance was afforded to obtain a variation in locations, particularly on the Gilberdyke to Doncaster section, which includes Goole. In this picture No 55016 heads the 1234 Hull-Kings Cross away from Goole on 18 April 1981. No 16 was the first Deltic to receive a General overhaul, emerging from Doncaster on 27 April 1976. Because it received extensive rewiring and inner body skin attention, it was the initial choice of the Deltic Preservation Society but it was not considered in the best of health, having suffered a small fire, and it worked its final train, the 1940 Kings Cross-Hull and ECS to York, on 23 December 1981. However, salvation finally came to *Gordon Highlander* by dint of the remarkable chance that it happened to be the final Deltic parked in the line awaiting scrapping and thus survived long enough to be purchased as the second locomotive of the 9000 Locomotive Limited. It was delivered to the Nene Valley Railway on 30 July 1984. *(Dave Stacey)*
Pentax MX Kodachrome 1/250, f4

Below. Hull was certainly put on the railway map in 1979 when the Deltics were entrusted with 'The Hull Executive', which at that time included the fastest schedule of a British train, the 91.4mph dash between Kings Cross and Retford. Prior to this, the Class 55s had frequently been rostered for 'The Hull Pullman', which ceased in May 1978. Here No 55002 departs from Hull Paragon with the 1630 to Kings Cross on 18 April 1981. Hull's final up Pullman train was worked by No 55014. *(Dave Stacey)*
Pentax MX Kodachrome 25 1/250, f4

Above. This picture taken at York in 1976 provides a reminder that all railway activity is transient and is already part of history, for the locomotives' headcode panels are either blanked-off or displaying the four '0s'. On the left is Class 47 No 47040 with a return excursion from York to Kings Cross whilst one of the Finsbury Park machines, No 55012 *Crepello*, waits to leave with the southbound 'Aberdonian' on 29 July 1976. *(Hugh Ballantyne)*
Leica M3 Kodachrome 25 1/250, f5.6

Right. Deltics on the Scarborough line became fairly common when the class was concentrated at York. The usual train to see Deltic haulage was the Scarborough-Kings Cross service which ran in the summer weeks. The train went ecs to Scarborough to form the 0954 return. In this view No 55006 *Fife and Forfar Yeomanry*, one of the early Deltics to meet its demise, crosses the River Derwent between Malton and Castle Howard with the 0954 from Scarborough on 13 September 1980. *(Hugh Ballantyne)*
Leica M3 Kodachrome 25 1/500, f2.8

Sunday morning outside Kings Cross was the time to be present to witness a procession of Class 55s leaving the terminus, for inward locomotives were utilised to take ecs workings to Ferme Park and Bounds Green. This view shows No 55004 *Queen's Own Highlander* removing the ecs of an overnight sleeper service past Holloway on 8 August 1981. *(Hugh Dady) Praktica IV Kodachrome 64 1/500, f4.5*

Oakleigh Park with No 55019 storming past at the head of the 1403 Kings Cross-York semi-fast service on 20 July 1981. Deltic engineers jokingly used to say that if you managed to get past Potters Bar without shedding a piston through the crankcase you would be alright for a good journey! No 55019 did get past Potters Bar on this occasion! In reality, shedding a piston was a very serious affair and one prominent engineer escaped death by seconds when he moved away from a crankcase just before an explosion in which a loose piston smashed through the engine and hurled itself through one of the Deltic's bodyside windows. *(Hugh Dady)*
Praktica IV Pentacon 200mm
Kodachrome 64 1/500, f5.6

Above. Although York depot had frequently given minor attention to Class 55 locomotives, it was not until May 1979 that it received Gateshead's and Haymarket's allocation and, with the closure of Finsbury Park as a maintenance depot on 31 May 1981, that depot's remaining allocation. The York depot staff immediately took a pride in their locomotives and personalised them with the York city coat of arms, for which permission was obtained from the 'city fathers'. With the end in sight for the class, York staff spent much time painting and cleaning the four Deltics earmarked for hauling the farewell specials – Nos 55002, 55009, 55015 and 55022. In this nocturnal view can be seen left to right Nos 55004, 55007 and 55015. The date was 20 December 1981 at which time No 4 had been condemned and was yielding spares to its sisters. *(Ian McCart)*
Praktica L2 Ektachrome 200 4 secs, f4

Right. No 55002 rests in its home depot, York, on 28 August 1981. This machine was one of four nominated on Thursday 10 September of that year by the CM&EE to work the 'Deltic Farewell' specials during the following autumn. The actual Deltics were chosen by the Regional Shopping Controller, Mr Jimmy Jewell, following an inspection of the survivors. However, No 2 was an inevitability in view of its green livery and planned preservation, although it succumbed during the night of 21 November, when it put a connecting rod through a crankcase. The Deltic towed No 55014 to Stratford where an operational unit from the latter was put into No 2 to enable it to continue in service until the end of the year. *(Hugh Dady)*
Praktica IV Kodachrome 64 10 secs, f5.6

Below. It was only in the latter years of the Deltics' reign on the ECML that the class ventured north of Edinburgh on a more regular basis. At no time were there any diagrams which officially took the class beyond the Scottish capital but with an abundance of HSTs and few diagrams left for the Deltics, Scottish Region Control made good use of the 55s by utilising them on Dundee/Aberdeen, Carstairs and, occasionally, Glasgow trains. This view depicts No 55002 crossing the Forth Bridge in charge of the 1700 Edinburgh-Aberdeen on 20 April 1981. (*Gavin Morrison*)
Pentax SP1000 Kodachrome 25 1/250, f3.5

Right. Another example of local Scottish Deltic working is this portrait of No 55012 *Crepello* accelerating off the Tay Bridge with the 0910 Dundee-Kings Cross on 13 September 1980. This train was the 1050 Edinburgh-Kings Cross, starting back at Dundee. At Haymarket depot the previous evening the photographer inquired which Deltic was likely to be allocated to work the train, there being four on shed from which to choose. "Which one would you like?" was the reply and as No 12 was the only one of the four with white window surrounds, this was duly chosen! They even cleaned it, but what else would you expect from Haymarket? (*Mrs D A Robinson*)
Pentax 6×7 Ektachrome 200 1/500, f6.3

Although the Class 55s made sporadic appearances at Bradford in the early years, it was not until the 1970s that the Deltics were everyday visitors and, of course, the prestige working was 'The Bradford Executive'. Leaving Bradford with a customary display of exhaust is No 55012 *Crepello* at the head of the 1730 to Kings Cross on 6 June 1978. (*John S Whiteley*)
Pentax SP2 Kodachrome 25 1/250, f3.5

The date of Tuesday 19 June 1979 was a notable one for the Class 55s, for on this day a Deltic set sail for Liverpool. No 55015 took 1M73 the 1128 Newcastle-Liverpool, through to its destination and everyone wondered why it had not been done sooner. This paved the way for regular sorties to Liverpool using York crews and this continued to the end of the Deltics' reign. This is No 55008 *The Green Howards* passing the site of the former steam shed at Mirfield on a York to Liverpool working on 20 October 1981. No 55008 survived until the end, its last service train being the 2120 Aberdeen-Kings Cross on 29 December 1981, and only flat batteries prevented it being used on the final service day, hauling the 1403 Kings Cross-York. Both power units from this machine, Nos 415 and 430 are owned by the Deltic Preservation Society and a cab from No 8 was purchased by Oxfordshire Deltic fan Paul Lambeth. *(Les Nixon)*

Pentax 6×7 Ektachrome 200

Below. A pictorial review of the Deltics would be incomplete without a scene on the Northumberland coast north of Berwick. This is No 55006 *Fife and Forfar Yeomanry* at Burnmouth heading the 0725 Plymouth-Edinburgh, which it took over at York. The date was 15 September 1979. By this time there were only eleven Deltic diagrams and only two daytime trains north of York, the 0550 Kings Cross-Aberdeen and the 0940 Edinburgh-Plymouth and return from York. (*Peter J Robinson*)
Pentax 6×7 Ektachrome 1/1000, f4

Right. As the HSTs took over more and more Deltic duties, by the last year, 1981, the class had been relegated to some humble duties, including the Newcastle-Edinburgh locals. No 55013, named *The Black Watch* at Dundee on 16 January 1963, winds round the Penmanshiel diversion on 8 June 1981 with the 1718 Edinburgh-Newcastle. No 55013 nearly made it to the end of the Deltic era but expired on 16 December 1981 whilst heading 1B26, the 0703 Peterborough-Kings Cross, and was condemned on 21 December. (*Mrs D A Robinson*)
Pentax 6×7 Ektachrome 200 1/1000, f4.5

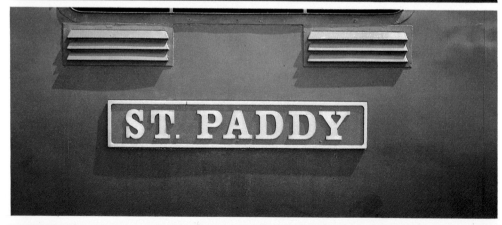

Top left. D9011's name was bestowed upon it at a ceremony held at Newcastle Central station on 28 May 1963. Memories of No 11 are recalled in this view taken on 21 May 1978 at Doncaster Works. (*Hugh Ballantyne*)
Leica M3 50mm Summicron Kodachrome 25 1/60, f4

Centre left. The naming of the Deltics was left to the three owning Regions. The Scottish and North Eastern both chose regimental names whilst the Eastern had the initiative to bestow tradition on its foremost machines with racehorse names, thus epitomising speed and grace. D9000 was named *Royal Scots Grey* at Edinburgh Waverley on 18 June 1962. This view was taken at York on 29 July 1976. (*Hugh Ballantyne*)
Leica M3 50mm Summicron Kodachrome 25 1/60, f4

Left. D9001 was the first Deltic to enter service, sister D9000 being delayed by power unit coolant problems. D9001, together with fellow Finsbury Park machine D9003, ran in service without nameplates, these being later fitted in Doncaster Works. D9001 had probably one of the finest names of the Deltic fleet and its memory will not fade. This was how it looked at Kings Cross on 10 July 1976. (*Gavin Morrison*)
Pentax SP1000 Kodachrome II 1/250, f3.5

Above. The winged thistle emblem, carried by 'The Flying Scotsman' in the early 1960s, epitomises more than any other device the reign of the Deltics. Made of fibreglass with a metal bracket behind, it was never carried by blue-liveried Deltics until the one owned by the National Railway Museum was specially loaned for certain final runs as the class ended its career. One thistle was kept at Finsbury Park depot and is shown adorning No 55003 *Meld* on 30 July 1977. (*Gavin Morrison*)
Pentax SP1000 Kodachrome II 1/250, f4

This was the sight which shocked and saddened all Deltic fans when the first Class 55 was broken up. Although Doncaster Works had gradually outshopped the numerous Deltics awaiting repaired power units (no fewer than 14 were in the Works on 19 October 1978) until just Nos 1 and 20 remained, the decision was taken on 18 December 1979 to condemn both machines in view of the number of man hours required to repair them. Both were officially withdrawn on 5 January 1980 and this sad view shows No 55020 *Nimbus* at the start of its scrapping on the same day with No 55001 *St Paddy* waiting its turn. Gone but not forgotten. *(Dave Stacey) Pentax KX Kodachrome 64 1/125, f6.5*

Above. With Deltics Nos 55001 and 55020 being the first to be cut up, photographs of these machines in service were considered by many as 'collectors items'! Indeed, before the final run-down began with the collosal and unprecedented interest shown by enthusiasts, not every Deltic train was photographed! This is No 55001 *St Paddy* in happier days before that fateful day on 24 March 1978 when it was switched off for the last time. *St Paddy* is heading south over Newark crossing on a wet day in August 1977 when the crossing hut was still standing. *(Hugh Ballantyne)*
Leica M3 Kodachrome 25 1/500, f2.8

Right. Despite its photographic qualities, the East Coast Main Line between Newcastle and Edinburgh was the least photographed when the Deltics held sway. No 55014 had just enjoyed a run over this 124¾-mile stretch when pictured approaching Newcastle at Shieldfield on 28 December 1976. The train was the 0955 Edinburgh-Kings Cross. *(Peter J Robinson)*
Pentax 6×7 Ektachrome 200 1/500, f5.6

Right. It was not until 1970 that the Deltics were authorised to be used on specials provided that operating requirements were not jeopardised. The late 1970s saw several members work deep into Western Region territory and on 26 March 1978 one notable Southern exploration took Finsbury Park's No 55007 *Pinza* on a tour of Kentish lines. Sporting a somewhat incongruous headboard, No 7 is pictured at Shortlands. There were many Deltic fans saddened that this machine was not saved for preservation. It expired whilst working the 0807 York-Kings Cross on 30 December 1981 and met its end in Doncaster Works in July 1982. (*R C Riley*)
Canon FTQL
Kodachrome 25
1/250, f4

Opposite. One of the most notable final excursions for the Class 55s took No 55002 from York to Swindon and Paddington on 28 November 1981. Here the train is pictured on its outward leg at Cudworth. On the front is carried the wooden headboard painted with D9000 in green livery. This board was kept by Vernon Broadhead, Traction Maintenance Engineer at York depot for many years, and is now displayed in the locomotive section in the RM&EE's office, Hudson House, York. (*Les Nixon*)
Pentax 6×7
Ektachrome 200
1/250, f6.3

Above. Dawn at Peterborough as the Class 55s enter their final weeks on 5 December 1981. On the left is No 55015 *Tulyar* at the head of 'The Hadrian Flyer' special and right No 55007 *Pinza* on the 0550 Kings Cross-Aberdeen. *Pinza* was the first Deltic to be modified to provide power for electric train heat, this being accomplished by tapping the main generator. One drawback of this arrangement was that the tapped power unit had to be worked harder to supply the required voltage and as a consequence the entire class was modified so that both power units supplied current when idling, but under full load the leading unit took over with the provision of eth current. (*Ian McCart*)
Praktica L2   Ektachrome 200   3 secs, f4

Right. BR had underestimated the extent of interest of Deltic afficionados in the final months and, to capitalise on the situation, advertised Deltic traction on two successive Sundays in the final weeks of BR service on scheduled Liverpool services. Deltics had become a familiar sight on the trans-Pennine run to Liverpool in the twilight years and not surprisingly the Sunday trains were packed. Pictured waiting in Liverpool Lime Street on Sunday 20 December 1981 with the 1910 to York is No 55022 *Royal Scots Grey*, suitably decorated by members of the York Railway Circle. (*Barry Plues*)
Pentax SP1000   Ektachrome 200   12 secs, f5.6

Funereal weather set the scene, somewhat appropriately, on the final service day of the Class 55s, 31 December 1981. There were only two Deltic departures from Kings Cross on that memorable day, the 0940 and 1603 stoppers to York. No 55008 should have worked the 1403 but was replaced by a Class 47 due to flat batteries. This picture shows the 0940 at Little Bytham behind No 55021, blazing into history on its last run. When it arrived at York, it was switched off never to run again. This Deltic had spent the last few weeks of its life running on one engine only, No 439, and this power unit is now one of those owned by the Deltic Preservation Society. (*Rodney Lissenden*)
Pentax 6×7 Ektachrome 200 1/500, f6.3

Right. The beautifully and tastefully regaled No 55019 after it had completed its last service run in BR ownership – the 1630 Aberdeen-York on 31 December 1981. These headboards had left Kings Cross adorning No 55017 that same evening on the 1603 to York, but after the train had been terminated at Grantham they were taken by HST to Darlington, where they were fitted to No 19 so that it could arrive at Deltic City, York, in style. The wreath belonging to the Deltic Preservation Society was duly carried on the farewell Deltic run two days later by No 55015 whilst the other headboards were carried by standby locomotive 55009. (*David Vickers*)
Pentax ME Super   Kodachrome 25
10 secs, f5.6

Below. Only two loyal Deltic fans in the country achieved the 'master shot' on the final farewell run on 2 January 1982 as No 15 heading the special passed No 9, the standby, at Newcastle. One took it in black and white and the other in colour and this is the latter! This was to be the start of an extraordinary saga for No 55015 before it was finally secured for preservation by Peter Sansom and moved to the Midland Railway Centre at Butterley. No 55009 was duly acquired by the Deltic Preservation Society after a phenomenal fund-raising effort and now sees regular use on the Moors Railway. What a way to remember these locomotives in BR service! (*David Vickers*)
Pentax ME Super   Kodachrome 25
1/125, f2.8

The end. Kings Cross station at 2030 on 2 January 1982, one of the most emotive days ever seen on the British railway scene. The fitting headboard 'Farewell to thy Greatness' had been manufactured by John Scott from Limekilns, Dunfermline. No 55022 had been seen by many thousands of people on its epic journey and, indeed, more people had turned out to pay their respects than for any steam special in living memory. The arrival at Kings Cross was even covered on national television news and depicted grown men in tears. *Royal Scots Grey* had arrived amid a tumultous welcome with its horn blaring throughout the length of the platform. At the same time, the standby locomotive, No 55009 *Alycidon*, was heading north from Peterborough to York for the last time and No 55022 followed in its footsteps, bringing to an end the most remarkable career of any diesel locomotive class in this country. *(Brian Cooke)*
Nikon EF
Ektachrome 200
1/15, f5.6

61

The two Deltic Preservation Society-owned Class 55s have fared excellently since purchase and have proved the sceptics wrong. The secret of preservation is not the purchase of the locomotive but the acquisition of spares, and the DPS has wisely invested in many components, including five power units. In addition, these five units had run the least engine hours of those available for sale and thus have years of life left in each of them. Here No 55019 *Royal Highland Fusilier* eases round Ellerbeck with the 1620 Pickering-Grosmont service on 2 July 1983. The only difficulty experienced with this Deltic to date has been the failure of one traction motor. *(Mrs D A Robinson)*
Pentax 6×7 Ektachrome 200 1/500, f6.3

No 55009 *Alycidon* heads the 1412 Goathland-Pickering DPS special, 'The Moors Explorer', near Ellerbeck on 12 May 1984. This locomotive had just received a repaint in 'Finsbury Park' blue. One of its main generators failed after a year in service but, like the traction motor defect on No 55019, was not the result of any neglect or lack of maintenance. This locomotive is held in much affection by many former Finsbury Park staff, some of whom regularly work on Nos 9 and 19. It was No 55009 which was specially selected and groomed by this depot to work the last Deltic-hauled train when Finsbury Park closed as a maintenance depot on 31 May 1981. *Alycidon* worked the 1605 Kings Cross-York with a commemmorative headboard 'Farewell Finsbury Park'. *(Peter J Robinson)*
Pentax 6×7 Ektachrome 200 1/500, f8

Royal Scots Grey now exercises itself at sporadic intervals on the Nene Valley Railway. Restored as No 9000 and maintained by members of the 9000 Locomotive Limited, future plans include repainting into two-tone green livery with the 'D' prefix re-instated. The Deltic now carries power units Nos 413, formerly in No 55012, and 434, latterly in No 55011. Here *Royal Scots Grey* is pictured during its first weekend of operation on the NVR and is seen backing onto its train at Orton Mere station on 23 October 1983. (*John Rudd*)

Mamiya 645 Agfachrome R100S 1/125, f8